The Truth
Is Beyond
Belief!

**Some thoughts to make you think
about the power of your thoughts...**

Jerry Durr

Mill City Press

Mill City Press, Inc.
2301 Lucien Way #415
Maitland, FL 32751
407.339.4217
www.millcitypress.net

Printed in the United States of America

ISBN-13: 9781545634110

PREFACE

My "Journey in Truth" began twenty years ago with an 8 part Television series called "The Long Search" which chronicled the major religions of the world. I was amazed at the diversity of beliefs about what, to my thinking, should be the same thing: the story of the source and sustenance of our existence. And when the documentary was over, despite the many differences, I was fascinated at seeing what I like to call the "samenesses" contained within all these religions.

An Eastern teaching from that series stated: "The One, when viewed from below, appears to be the many. The many, when viewed from above, is seen to be The One." This "lofty" perspective has, to this day, inspired me to explore the power and role of the human mind with its magical ability to so seamlessly impose its own subjective, separating beliefs overtop an objective, unified reality - Existence Itself.

On my journey I have enjoyed studying some great teachers and great teachings. There are so many aspects to know about The Infinite with its seeming contradictions that it reminds me of the three blind men describing the large elephant only according to the small portions that they each had touched. And so, man is continually doing his best to describe The Infinite in finite terms. Each attempts to put a unique "spin" on the unfathomable truth of our existence so that it might be better understood by others.

The words contained herein are the product of many years of looking outward at the miracle of physical life, and looking deeply within at the mystery of thought and consciousness. The sometimes paradoxical formulation of these thoughts and ideas are presented for quiet contemplation with the intention of helping dislodge the mind from its somewhat fixed positioning. They are meant to be taken in and absorbed by the intellect, but they will be most helpful if they are read and felt from the heart.

I have never heard of an earnest Truth seeker who returned to say "don't come this way, stay back with your illusions." The "Truth that sets us free" is that our only problems are our illusions. May your own journey dispel your illusions, leading you to Truth, clarity, deep inner peace and the joyful realization that God really is love, and Love really is all there is.

TABLE OF CONTENTS

Chapter 1
The Extraordinariness of Ordinariness 11
Man's most amazing ability: to overlay the extraordinariness
of his existence with his perceptions of its ordinariness.

Chapter 2
The Beginning of Man 33
The birth of separate, separating thought. Man's journey
from his Everythingness into his thoughts of somethingness.

Chapter 3
The Pattern Holders of Life 55
What the world is made of: God's pattern holders of energy
and matter; man's pattern holders of thought and belief.

Chapter 4
Past, Present, Future 77
The mind's creations of the past and future; God's creation
of the present.

Chapter 5
Illusion 99
Man's ever-changing, subjective creations of thought
and belief.

Chapter 6
Truth. 121
The wonderful Truth of existence; that which remains
after our thoughts and beliefs have been set aside.

Chapter 7
Free Will and Destiny 143
The paradox of free will and destiny; seeing that our
destiny is the result of our free will choices.

Chapter 8
The Ending of Man. 163
The Ascension, the Awakening, The Atonement; the
mind's surrendering back into The Unified Thought.

Chapter 9
Love. 175
The greatest miracle is Life Itself, but the most
wonderful miracle is that Love is Its source.

Chapter 10
The Magic of God and Man .199
God and man each create something from nothing.
God has created the world; man is creating his thoughts and
beliefs about the world.

CHAPTER 1

The Extraordinariness of Ordinariness

Perhaps...
The
Most
Extraordinary
Thing
About
Life
Is
Its
Ordinariness...

*This absolutely
Extraordinary World,
This absolutely
Extraordinary Experience
called Life,
is so completely obscured
by the single thought
that it's all
just so ordinary.
How extraordinary !*

Maybe...
The only reason
we don't see
the extraordinariness
of life
is because we have been,
for such a long time,
judging it to be
so ordinary...

*We have unwittingly
been defining this truly
extraordinary experience
as being just ordinary,
and so that is exactly
what it has become !*

The greatest miracle
that could ever happen to
ANYONE
has already happened to
EVERYONE !
If you're breathing,
you've got it !

Cling tightly
to The Miracle that
YOU ARE !

*Using the absolute highest
of all logical thinking,
All of Life
– including God –
should never have happened !
But,
to our absolute good fortune,
it did !*

*Cling tightly
to The Miracle that
YOU ARE !*

This Truly
Extraordinary Experience
is not only a
"once in a lifetime miracle,"
This Truly
Extraordinary Experience
is a
"once in Eternity miracle."

Cling tightly
to The Miracle that
YOU ARE !

*We should all
stop quibbling about
how
The Universe
came into existence,
and just drink deeply of
the fact that,
against infinite odds,
It did !*

*Cling tightly
to The Miracle that
YOU ARE !*

*Such a gossamer thin film
of ordinary thoughts
keep you from
continually remembering
the greatest of all miracles;
that, against
truly extraordinary odds,
Existence exists –
You exist !*

*Cling tightly
to The Miracle that
YOU ARE !*

*Because
you do not realize
the amazing fact
of what you truly are,
you have been
imagining yourself
to be what
you truly are not.
Can you imagine this ?*

*Because
you have forgotten
what you truly are,
as a limitless expression of
The Infinite,
you have been trading your
"Everythingness"
for a few paltry thoughts
of
"somethingness."*

If you look deeply within
you may be surprised to find
that you have
never actually been
what you have
always thought you were.

In fact,
you will see that
you are really
so much more.

The irony is that
we usually don't have
enough imagination
to see Reality.

This is because
we usually can't imagine
that there can actually be
much of anything
beyond what
we can imagine.

*For the purpose of
your endless experiencing;
"Who You Are"
(as a person)
is ever-changing.*

*For the purpose of
your Eternal safekeeping;
"What You Are"
(as pure Spirit)
is never-changing.*

Being a Perfect Creator,
in Whose image
You are made,
it can be very difficult
for You to ultimately see
that what You really are
is the pure and unchanging
Awareness
behind the
ever-changing creations
of your own mind.

How extraordinary...
To see that what
You really are is The Pure
and Changeless Awareness,
beyond thought,
that has become identified
with the ever-changing
thoughts themselves.

You are like the changeless
beam from the projector
that has become identified
with the ever-changing
stream of pictures for which
it is merely providing the light.

We extraordinary creatures,
being both body and mind,
stand awesomely positioned
with a foot in two worlds.

We are neither just Spirit
that has no effect
on matter,
nor just matter
that has no effect
on Spirit.

We occupy the very special
location at the crossroads
of these two worlds.

*Being comprised of
both matter and Spirit means
you are a finite being
having an experience
of The Infinite
and
You Are The Infinite
having an experience
as a finite being.*

*You are a physical being
having a Spiritual experience
and
You Are a Spiritual Being
having a physical experience.*

*God
has never really
wanted any of us to do
anything other than
enjoy both His and our
creations.*

*But it seems we have
become so hopelessly lost
in our own creations
that we are now
almost completely
missing His.*

I used to
"Think"
life was all physical,
now I
"See"
life is all mental.

I used to
"Think"
I was in the world,
now I
"See"
the world is in me.

CHAPTER 2

The Beginning of Man

In the beginning
(of separativity)
was the thought,
with its capacity to
seemingly separate.

And the creator of
individuating thought
became
the creator of
(the perception of)
separation.

The pivotal
"Beginning of Man"
was not only
the individual body,
but especially
the individuating mind.

And with this mind
could come endless thoughts
of individuation.

And because these thoughts
could become (held within) flesh,
the creator (of flesh)
could become the embodiment
of his own individuating
thoughts.

The mystical
"Beginning of Man"
was the descent
from
"Complete Knowingness"
into
"limited perception,"
from
"Everythingness"
into
"somethingness,"
from
"The Reality of Oneness"
into
"the illusion of separateness."
The descended is individual.
The Ascended is indivisible.

*The world of perceived
barriers and separations
is more than it appears.*

*The most powerful of
barriers and separations
are not made of matter,
but of thoughts and beliefs.*

*The real separating element
of Existence
is more commonly known as
"mind."*

It appears that your thoughts
can separate The Inseparable.
Example:
as long as you think
GOD
and
The Universe
are separate
you will have a perception
of your own making,
a perception appearing
as a separation
of The Inseparable.

*It appears that
individual thought
is the product of
the separate self.*

*In fact,
the separate self
is the product of
individuating thoughts.*

*The only time or place
there has ever been
(the illusion of)
aloneness
has been in the mind.*

*In fact,
the mind of man
is a marvel made expressly
to create and experience
(the illusion of)
being alone.*

*Your every boundary
is but the result
of a conclusion
that you,
alone,
have made about
being alone.*

*All that you
have ever been,
as a person,
you have been
in your thoughts alone.*

*With your most amazing
memory and imagination
you have created a
"picture of the world"
about which now
are all of your questions.*

*Thoughts are the
building blocks of the self.
You have become
a walking depository
of your thoughts about life.*

*"Just who do you
think you are ?"
really does describe your
process of self-creation.*

*Thoughts
are also your navigator,
taking you in to,
or keeping you out of,
any experience
you can think of.*

We sometimes think
that we can find God
in our thoughts.

In fact,
our thoughts and beliefs
are the only things
that have ever separated us
from God.

God is not found
in our thoughts,
God is found in the space
between and beyond
our thoughts.

*In fact,
we have never been
separated from God,
each other, or the world
by anything thicker
than a single thought.*

*And that
is the thought
that we really are
(and really want to be)
separate.*

*Thought
is an amazing tool
with the ability to seemingly
separate the inseparable.
In fact,
there has never been
a separating device
other than thought.
And when the
separating thought
is removed,
it becomes clear
there has never really been
anything that was separate.*

*In Reality
there is no problem.*

*This is because
there is no real separation
outside of what
we think and believe.*

*To our
absolute good fortune:
The Truth
(of our oneness)
Is Beyond Belief
(of our separation)!*

*You may think
that if you were to
suspend or discard your
self-created,
self maintained
thoughts about yourself
that you would find
you are nothing.*

*In fact,
you will see that
You Are Everything.*

How the separations occur:
the degree that you
judge another person
as desirable or undesirable
is the same degree to which
you separate them
from yourself.

And the degree that you
judge youself better or worse
than another person
is the same degree to which
you separate yourself
from them.

*The critical thing
that separates you
from God, other people,
experiences or
states of being
is the thought
that you are separate.*

*And realize that
a single thought
separates you as completely
as a thousand thoughts.*

Realize that
The Infinite
is not trying to stand out
and be separate
from you.

Realize it is you
who are trying to stand out
and be separate
from The Infinite.

Our major dilemma
lies not in seeing
that we are different,
our major dilemma
lies in thinking
that we are separate.

But to our
absolute good fortune:
The Truth
(of our oneness)
Is Beyond Belief
(of our separation)!

Look beyond all of the
Apparent separations
And you will see that

GOD

AND the

YOUniverse

ARE so

ONEderful.

CHAPTER 3

The Pattern Holders of Life

*All of life
is but the endless
and wonderful play
of "pattern holders"
and "patterns held."*

*The atom, the Adam,
and the Universe
could happen only after
God discovered a way to
"create and hold a pattern."*

*Everything
from the electron,
to the gene, to the mountain,
to the passing cloud
is but energy
holding a particular pattern.*

*Entropy
– continual transformation –
is the saving grace
of Existence.
Without Entropy
all patterns would
remain forever locked
in their particular state.*

*Man,
like an island,
continually tries
to maintain his
"fixed positioning"
in a Universe that,
like a river,
is forever flowing.*

*The physical world
is the ultimate form of
"pattern holding,"
while
the human mind/brain
is The Master at
"pattern recognition."
Each is there for the other
and each is,
in fact,
the perfect complement
for the other.*

Thought affects matter,
matter affects thought.

This is the
"Play of Existence."

The sculptor affects
the piece of granite
with his creative thought,
and the sculpture,
in turn,
affects the thoughts
of all those who view it.

Every thought is a created,
creative pattern of energy.

With each of our definitions
we fashion energy into
a unique "thought form."

Once stored in our body/brain,
each thought stands ready
to create and implement its
respective pattern
or be replaced with yet
another creative pattern.

*Just as the computer
so accurately stores
the encoded programs
that provide its
"operating system,"
so does our body/brain
accurately store the
many thoughts and beliefs
that become our personal
"operating systems."*

*The body/brain is such a
wondrous device for storing,
enacting, and especially feeling
our thoughts and ideas.*

We, like the computer,
are so "flexibly inflexible."
It's not our physical patterns
that cause our illness
and unhappiness,
for they are but effects.
It is our rigid mental patterns
that are the cause.

The primary requirement for
health and happiness is the
letting go of all the patterns
that are causing our
dis-ease and unhappiness.

Pain is physical,
suffering is mental.

Both are but the result
of patterns held
too tightly
or too long.

Difficulties arise when,
from such a limited and
subjective point of view,
we so strongly insist
on how long each of life's
ever-changing patterns
should last.

In doing so,
we fail to see
the ever present
perfection
in the pattern holding rates
of the cloud, the flower,
the kitten or the mountain.

Suffering
is but the result
of our inability
to see and accept
the perfect
rates of change in the
patterns of life.

Prolong not the past,
hasten not the future,
and just see the perfection
contained within
the patterns of the present.

*Come to love and marvel
at the diversity and beauty
of all of the patterns
that make up your life.*

*Just be sure to hold them
gently enough
to allow them
their continual
transformations.*

*Convictions
are the grandfather
of all our
pattern holding
mechanisms,
being constructed of our
preferences, aversions,
hopes and fears.*

*Addiction
is our most extreme form
of pattern holding,
being the result
of a personal conviction
that our
long-chosen patterns
now hold us.*

It is both our
pattern making ability
and our
pattern holding ability
that are so powerful.

This is because
love, fear, and reason
are the formidable forces
behind both
our pattern making
and
our pattern holding.

Seeing all of life
as a play of
pattern holders
and
patterns held
resolves our sometimes
seeing it as a problem,
and allows us
to simply become aware
of the endless patterns
that we are choosing to
hold and behold.

What we call finding
Love, Peace or Joy
is but the result of
interrupting or releasing
the pattern holding forces
of fear, anger and guilt.

While these forces
are not stronger than
Love, Peace or Joy,
they do have the ability
to render them obscure.

Love, Peace and Joy
are the natural results
of choosing
to not create any new
— or maintain any old —
patterns
that would in any way
keep these things from us.

Consider that...
God's thinking
regulates the relatively
fixed and changing patterns
of the Universe,
like our own thinking
regulates the relatively
fixed and changing patterns
of our personal lives.

*After seeing
that all of life
is the play of pattern holders,
turn your attention to
that mysterious part of you
which can create,
hold and observe patterns.*

*And turn your attention
to the magical patterns
that You are now creating,
holding and beholding.*

CHAPTER 4

Past, Present, Future

*The past
is a product
of the memory.*

*The future
is a product
of the imagination.*

*The Present
is the product
of Reality.*

*So much of our life is
the product of the memory
and the imagination.*

*These are the instruments
we use to create
anger, guilt, worry and fear.*

*And these are the only things
that can remove us from
the Peace and Perfection
of The Present.*

*Anger and guilt
come from memories
about the past.*

*Fear and worry
come from imaginings
about the future.*

*Peace and Perfection
come from
resting completely
in The Present.*

*Difficulties arise from
con-fusing
(negatively fusing)
The Present
with the past or future.
Without anger or guilt
about the past,
or fear or worry
about the future,
only the
Peace and Perfection
of The Present
will remain.*

*When we can see that
neither past nor future
are actually real
in The Present,
and that
The Present
is the only thing
that is ever actually real;
we will also see that
neither anger nor fear
are ever actually real
except in the moments
we choose to "real-ize" them:
make them real to ourselves.*

Anger, guilt, fear, worry,
have always been
of our own making,
while Peace and Love
are of God's.

We are creating an imperfect
past and future in our minds,
while God has created
The Perfect Present
in Reality.

Reality is Now.

Reality is Perfect.

*It is only our thoughts
about Its imperfection
(our fantasies)
that prevent us from
continually seeing this.*

The Perfection of Reality
is always present,
and
is always a present,
whether
we can see it or not.

*It is mainly our judgements
about past and future
that separate us from
The Present Reality of God.*

*Anger is a judgement about
what happened in the past;
fear is a judgement about
what we think will happen
in the future.*

*We can so completely
separate ourselves from
The Present Perfection
of Reality
with something as unreal as
an angry or fear-full thought.*

*The secret
of realizing how
Adam felt on the
"morning of creation"
is to remember the
"presence of mind"
(mind in the present)
he was experiencing
before he created
any thoughts about
past or future.*

Man often uses his
thoughts about
past and future
like a child uses his toys:
to fill in the seeming
"unsatisfactoriness"
of the present moment.

*Choose not
to let the pricelessness
of a present,
peace-filled mind
be intruded upon
by nonsensical thoughts
about the past and future.*

*In The Present
is the present
of Perfect Peace.*

*Our thoughts about
the past and future
cannot affect
the perfection of
The Present.*

*But they can,
and most certainly do,
affect the way
we see and experience
this perfection.*

The Present Reality
is always
perfect, pristine,
silent, unspeakable.

We need only stop
impressing upon it
our thoughts about
the past and future
in order to see this
ever-present Perfection.

A clear day

isn't

the most important thing

to see

The Perfection of Reality,

a clear mind is.

When
we can look upon
The Present Moment
without
assistance or hindrance
from our
"mental modifiers"
made of a past and future,
we will see the miracle of
Its Eternal Perfection.

*In Reality
there is only Now!*

*Your experience has never been
anywhere other than Now.*

*All pasts and futures
are but different viewpoints
of this same, one Now.*

*Every moment is actually
the same, Eternal Now
fractured by your thoughts
about difference and separation.*

In this moment;
Be happy that YOU ARE !

The Truly Wonderful Thing
isn't that you are "this"
or that you are "that",
The Truly Wonderful Thing
is that YOU simply ARE.

Rest completely in this
Priceless, Immutable,
Wonderful Truth.

Reality is Now.
Reality is Perfect.

For this moment,
leave your thoughts
about past or future,
and simply celebrate
The Perfection of The Now
and
The Perfection in The Now.

God

has already given us

the prefect present:

The Perfect Present.

Past, Present, Future

CHAPTER 5

Illusion

"Illusion"
means that something
is not actually
as we think it to be.
The world is an illusion
because it is not actually
the way we think it is.
In fact,
it is only our thoughts
that keep us from seeing
the unspeakable miracle
that it actually is.

This life truly is a dream.
And the major illusion
is that we see ourselves as
characters within this dream
instead of the Truth that
we are the dream's creator.

If our dream seems hellish
it is only because we
have not yet chosen
to create a dream
of Heaven.

*Everything was
"fine"
until we started to
"de-fine."*

*We have created our own
"definitions of the world"
about which now
are all of our questions.*

*This is why
"we are not in the world,"
it is actually that
"the world is in us."*

The moment we decide
"This is the way it is"
we have created a
"film of perception"
through which
we will view Reality.
But the perfection of Reality
is untouchable,
remaining as it was
before our self-created
"thought film",
and as it will be
when we withdraw our
defining ideas.

*We are often convinced
that our personal
"definitions of the world,"
gained through
experience, reason,
and understanding,
are correct and proper;
while the other person's
"definitions,"
gained through
the same process,
are where the
"problems of the world"
lie.*

*We think that
to destroy our personal
"definitions of the world"
(our beliefs)
would be a tragedy.*

*In fact,
all tragedy
is but the result
of our personal
"definitions."*

*Man
struggles diligently
to free himself
from a prison
that he, alone,
has created.*

*This prison has no bars,
but is constructed only
of his illusory thoughts,
definitions and beliefs.*

"Thought brick"
by
"thought brick,"
judgement
by
judgement,
we unwittingly create the
"brick wall of the mind"
that inevitably
separates us from the world.

*We do not realize
how we have so steadily
forged a prison
out of our own
fears, desires and beliefs.*

*Neither do we see
how powerfully
these illusory thoughts
now keep us constrained.*

*One source of illusion
arises from the fact
that because our
personal thoughts
sometimes coincide
with Truth,
we come to think
that all of our
personal thoughts
are true.*

The difficulty
isn't that the ego
is only a collection
of personal beliefs.
The difficulty is that
one of the ego's beliefs

is that
all of its beliefs
are real and true.

*Think
what you will about
fear, anger, worry or guilt.
But know
that your thoughts
will be real
only to the extent
that you make them so.*

*Take a moment
to stop and think about
the power of thought,
and just how well
your illusory thoughts
have been separating you
from the world and
the people of the world.*

*Realize that
You did not
come from your thoughts,
but your thoughts
are coming from you.*

*Your thoughts
did not create you,
but you are
creating your thoughts.*

*It can be helpful to see
the source of our two
major illusions:
fear and anger.*

*Fear comes from the way we
"think things are."
Anger comes from the way we
"think things should be."*

*When we stop creating these
ever-changing points of view,
we will enjoy the return to
life's peace and perfection.*

*We can fail to see
that our illusory
thoughts about Reality
are real only while
we are making them so
(real-izing them).*

*While
The Perfection of Reality
is always present
whether we realize it
or not.*

*It's so amazing
how completely
we can overlay
the perfection and unity
of Reality
with our illusory thoughts
about its imperfection
and separation.
Hence,
we cannot love a world
that we have deemed
unlovable or separate.*

Sometimes...
It's not
"what you believe"
that's important,
it's what you
"stop believing"
that's important.

Because sometimes...
It is only your beliefs
that keep you from seeing
what's really important;
that, against infinite odds,
YOU ARE !

Heaven and hell
lie not outside your mind.

While
Heaven
contains the knowing
that it is only you
who put yourself
in hell,
hell contains the belief
that Heaven cannot be here;
that Heaven cannot be now.

Truth
cannot contain illusion;
illusion
cannot contain Truth.

The Truth of What You Are
lies safe and secure
beyond the illusions of
what you think you are.

Know this Truth
and you will see
that you have always
been set free.

CHAPTER 6

Truth

*The
Truth
Is
Beyond
Belief !
The Truth of What You Are
remains forever
pure, pristine, perfect,
safely beyond the illusions
of what you may think you are.
Thank God this is The Truth,
whether you believe it or not.*

*Truth
is so beautiful.*

*But you can
fail to see this
when you become
too occupied
looking at your illusions.*

The Truth
that
"sets you free"
is but
the realization
that it is only
your illusions
(beliefs)
that have ever
imprisoned you.

Truth – Reality
is simply "what is."
Illusion – fantasy
is what you think
about "what is."

This Truth –
This Reality
is that which remains
just as It is
whether you believe in it
or not.

Truth
does not need your belief
in order to make It real,
while this is fantasy's
important requirement.

But fantasies
can never actually be real.
Fantasies
can only seem real
in the moments you are
trying to make them so.

*Realize that
you believe implicitly
in your own beliefs.*

*Also
realize that
The
Truth
Is
Beyond
Your
Beliefs !*

Just as a rock
cannot affect the Sun
but it can block its light;
So, you cannot affect
The Truth of What You Are
but you can certainly deny it.

A single illusory thought
about what you are not
can totally obscure
the most amazing Truth
of what you have always been.

*It's an illusion
to think that
Truth, Happiness, Heaven,
can be found anywhere
outside of yourself.*

*Truth, Happiness, Heaven
are not only within you;
Truth, Happiness, Heaven
Are You.*

*The one and only thing
that is not an illusion
is You.*

*But it may be difficult
for you to see this
Truth
because of the tight focus
you have been holding
on all of your illusions.*

Seeing
God - Truth - Reality
is all a matter of focus.

When you are focused
on the world
God won't seem real.

If you will focus on God
you'll see the world isn't real.

Strive to see only The Real.

*You don't see God
because you are only seeing
your own thoughts.*

*In Truth,
there is nothing
that is not God.*

*But you think
you are seeing only
a cloud, a flower,
a puppy, or a person.*

*In order to maintain
your personal illusions
you've had to surrender
your Truth.*

*Now,
in order to find your Truth,
you must surrender
your illusions.*

*But since illusions
can never be real,
realize that nothing
will actually be lost.*

You need not,

you cannot,

create Truth;

you need only,

you can only,

stop creating illusions.

See the mind
as being your collection
of thoughts and beliefs
through which you will
—by design—
view the world.

Clear away this
"cataract of the mind,"
with all of its illusory ideas,
and you will see
The Eternal Perfection
that it has so effectively
been blocking from your view.

*A belief
is always your own creation
of how you think life is,
or should be.*

*An angry, fearful adult
is full of these;
a carefree, joyful child
is free of these.*

*Fortunately,
The Truth
really is
Beyond your Beliefs.*

Love,
Joy,
Peace,
Truth
arise naturally
in the mind
unfettered by
fear,
desire,
judgement,
or illusion.

The reason
it can be so difficult
to find Truth
is because
the one thing you think
can reveal it to you,
the mind,
is so completely occupied
with its illusions.

When you think about
your thoughts long enough
they can become true to you.

Your difficulties arise
when you then mistake
these thoughts
for Truth.

God's creation
– Truth –
doesn't need correcting;
only your perception
of His creation
does.

The life of Enlightenment
and Truth
really is beyond belief.

It is a life of
freedom and knowing;
without need of special beliefs.

The Perfection of Existence
is recognized as far beyond,
and standing clear of,
any of the mind's ideas.

CHAPTER 7

Free Will and Destiny

*This amazing
Universe
gave you free will
because It knew It had
The Infinite capability
to support
whatever dream
you could imagine
(image-in).*

*Recognizing destiny
is recognizing the
"pattern holding"
quality of the soul.*

*See that even
the gentlest soul
maintains
the most powerful will;
the will of God.*

*It is helpful to realize
that all things are
in your life only because
you placed them there
and, more importantly, are
choosing to keep them there.*

*You bring everything into
your life because of your
preferences, aversions,
and the way they
"create you to be."
And they will stay only as
long as you choose them.*

*In this world
it is helpful to
keep in mind
two key elements:
destiny and karma.*

*They are actually
one and the same;
living out the results
of your "free will" choices.*

Understand
that when it seems
you have lost
your freedom of choice
it is only because
of your
lifetime(s)
of free will choices
that you have
already made.

*Have you
ever considered
how your accumulating
definitions and judgements,
preferences and priorities,
might be
— by design —
being stored within
the body/mind;
thereby literally
"incarnating your tendencies"
for the rest of this life,
and
perhaps the next?*

The road to Heaven
is paved with
good intentions.

Never stop intending
to be higher, brighter,
more loving, more caring,
more peaceful, more truthful,
more joyful, and more content.

Realize that the
guiding force of your life
has never been other
than your intentions.

*Mystics and Sorcerers
are said to move into
other worlds by
"fixing their intention"
there.*

*We choose to stay
in this world by
"fixing our intentions"
here.*

The journey of this life
is but exploring
the endless ways of
energizing and activating
the body with
the power of thought.

The physical body is,
without doubt,
the most amazing instrument
for the feeling and actuating
of non-physical
thoughts and ideas
that has ever been thought of.

*The moment you say
"what a great idea,"
you start the conditions
for The Universe
to bring it into
physical reality.*

*Great ideas don't just
happen to you;
great ideas,
more correctly,
happen through you.*

*Prayer
is not only for God,
for He already knows
your every thought;
prayer is more
importantly for the self,
showing you
what you now intend
to be, do or have.*

*You will always be, do or have
that which you most value,
because this is the force that
brings everything forth.*

*First,
become aware of your
"personal vision"
and then let it
do all of the work.*

*The energizing force
behind everyone's life
has never been anything
other than this.*

*One of man's greatest
personal understandings
might be understanding
why other people don't/can't
understand what he now
so clearly understands.*

*One explanation is that
"until you understand something
you just can't understand it."*

*By such marvelous design
we are each firmly held
within the confines
of our own understandings.*

*It's not that we
don't want to be happy,
for this is the root of all life.*

*It's that we keep
desiring the things
that offset our happiness
and avoiding the things
that will make happiness
ours.*

The primary requirement

for happiness

is but the letting go

of all the thoughts

that are causing

unhappiness.

God, Truth, Love, Light;

the more you seek It,

the more you see It;

the more you see It,

the more you seek It.

We

could all be

in Heaven

today,

if only

we hadn't

made other plans.

*Let us each choose
the God-given qualities of
Awareness,
Compassion,
Contentment,
Fulfillment,
Goodness,
Happiness,
Joy,
Love,
Mercy,
and Peace;
not only as our destination,
but also as our main journey.*

CHAPTER 8

The End of Man

The "End of Man,"
The "Atonement,"
the end of individuality,
is but
the realization that
everything he thought
to be separate
has always been
inseparable.

The "End of Man,"
The "Ascension,"
is but
rising into the awareness
that the part of him
that allows him to
"think"
he is a separate human,
is neither separate
nor human.

The "End of Man,"
The "Awakening,"
is but
the dreamer realizing that
there is no further need
to correct the dream;
the only requirement
is to awaken.

*The high cost
of man's
intense, continual
dreaming
is the inability
to ever consider
the ultimate goal
of awakening.*

*The "End of Man"
is but
the new understanding that
he has never actually been
what he always
"thought"
he was.*

*This heralds the
wonderful return
from his physical
"somethingness"
back to his Spiritual
"Everythingness."*

*Perhaps
it's not that man will
"Stand before God on his
final judgement day,"
but that he will
"Stand before God
(finally be able to see God)
on the day that he makes
his final judgement."*

*He will realize that
his personal judgements
(about men and God)
were the only things
that kept him from
"seeing God"
all along.*

Could the Genesis 3:3 scripture:
"Of all of the fruits you may
freely eat, except of the
'Tree of knowledge
of good and evil',
for then shall you die"
be speaking of an inevitable
phase of man's intellectual
evolution when he comes to
"think" he knows enough to
judge what is good and bad
by himself?

Are we not now dying
(killing each other)
over what we each think we
"know" to be good and evil?

The "End of Man"
comes with his choice
to stop creating a dream
of such specialness
and separation.

This decision reveals
that he was separate
only because of his
intense desire to be so,
to create his own separate
and separating dream.

In order to
"See God"
man must first
bring to a close
his personal collection of
beliefs about God.

For then will he see
that they were actually
the primary obstacles to
"Seeing God"
in the first place.

In the beginning
man comes to realize
the primary role
he plays in the creating
of his personal dream.

Then he sees how strongly
he has been holding
this dream in place.

And, most wonderfully,
in the end is his awareness
that he can now
make the choice to awaken.

The "End of Man"
comes with his choice
to stop creating dreams
of separation and
incompleteness.

This final choice
will lead him to see that
God is Peace,
God is Fullness,
and
God is Peace-Fullness.

CHAPTER 9
Love

LOVE

IS

FOR

GIVING

God Is Love,

God Is Light,

God Is Truth,

God Is Beauty,

God Is.

Love,
Light,
Truth,
Beauty,
come only where welcome;
against your will
they cannot enter.

Love is not learned;
Love is intrinsic,
it is your natural state.

It is hate that is an
acquired perspective.

In fact,
hate comes from anger
and anger comes from hurt.

The need is not
to create Love;
the need is to only
stop creating hate and anger,
and allow Love
to return on its own.

We often confuse
like and Love.

Like is physical,
Love is spiritual.

Like is a preference
and is a product of the mind,
while Love is total acceptance
and comes from the heart.

Like is what we acquire,
it is of our personal choosing;
Love is at our core,
it is what we are.

*Perhaps Love
Really Is all there is.*

*For what is fear
but a perception of losing
what we have come to love?
And what is anger
but a reaction to that
which is thwarting
what we have come to love?
And what is guilt
but feeling bad about
an experience
that we have so loved?*

*If you have an unloving
relationship with someone
it is not really the other
person's fault.*

*You may not be able
to keep the other
from not loving you,
but you can keep yourself
from not loving them.*

It's not

"loving"

that hurts;

it's

"not loving"

that hurts.

For such a long time
we have been making
so many other choices.
Now, to return home:

WE must choose Love,

We MUST choose Love,

We must CHOOSE Love,

We must choose LOVE.

In this life,
it's not
"who"
we are loving
that's important,
it's
"that"
we are loving
that's important.

Let us each

Choose Love,

Teach Love,

Be Love.

Remembering that

Always,

and in All ways,

we can trust Love.

The Divine plan:

*The
more
Loving
you
become,
The
more
Lovely
the world
becomes.*

The
Greatest Miracle
to ever happen
is Life Itself.

But the most
ONEderful Miracle
to ever happen
is that
Love is Its Source.

Just as white
is not the absence of color
but is the totality
of all colors,
So,
the Ecstatic feeling of Love
is not the absence
of some human emotions
but is the totality
of every emotion
that a human can feel.

The reason
Love feels so
ONEderful
is because
when you are
"in Love"
you are not just
feeling some of life,
you are feeling
all of life,
all at once.

*The reason you do not
love a person, or the world,
is usually because they
do not fill the role that you
have assigned to them.*

*But True Love,
being total acceptance,
is to cast aside your
self-made assignments,
in recognition of their
subjective limitations,
and just see each for the
wonderfully unique qualities
that they already have.*

Love
is
All That Is
and
Love
is
The All,
that Is.

Coming
into
The Light
is
coming
into
Delight;
coming
into
Delight
is
coming
into
The Light.

*Love
is not our creation,
Love
is God's creation.*

*Hate, anger, guilt and fear
are our creations.*

*And although our creations
can have no real affect
on Love,
they can block our awareness
to Its continual presence,
and Its continual presents.*

*You
cannot change the world,
for it is but the effect
of everyone.*

*But your choice
to become more loving
will change the way
that you see the world.*

*And in changing the way
you see the world,
you will have, in effect,
changed the world.*

Love

knows It contains

everything It needs

to be, create, and have,

more of whatever

It Loves.

Love

sees

The Good

and

The God

in everyone

and everything.

God

<u>Really Is</u>

Love

(pass it on)

CHAPTER 10

The Magic of God and Man

*The magical ability
of God and man
is very similar:
they both have created
something out of nothing.
God has created
the physical world
out of nothing
and man has created
his mental world
out of nothing.*

*Understand that
physically
you did not create yourself,
nor did you create the world
that you are looking at.*

*But mentally
you are creating
both yourself,
as who you think you are,
and the world
that you are seeing.*

*Perhaps
man's most important
understanding
lies in the realization
that his happiness
does not come from
the world he is looking at,
his happiness
comes from the world
that he is seeing.*

*In this physical world
man has never
really had control,
he has only had
the illusion of control.*

*What man does have
is a far more important
ability:
that of choice,
the choice of how
he wants to see this world.*

Just as there is
but a single sunbeam
shining through the
many different facets of
a stained glass window;
So, there is only
One Eternal Light
shining through
(giving life to)
the endless creations
of Existence.
The Life Force within
the atom and the elephant
is not separate nor different.

*The first
most unfathomable thing
about this miraculous Existence
is that
"Everything"
is actually
"The Same One Thing."*

*The second is how
"The Same One Thing"
has,
to such an intricate degree,
become
"The Everything!"*

*All of life
is actually but the
"play of great ideas."*

*In fact,
it's not that there are
"great people,"
it's that
there are people
who discover
and maintain
"great ideas."*

*Man's
greatest achievement
may lie in
getting his limited mind
to understand
just how unlimited
it actually is.*

The Eternal Essence
that is always present
within you
has been so perfectly
transparent, still and silent
that you have probably
never even noticed It.

At your core is the
Changeless Point of Awareness
around which
everything else is moving,
changing, living and dying.

This Awareness is not relative
to everything; everything
is relative to this Awareness.

God has created
The Real, The Eternal;
man is creating
the unreal, the ephemeral.

God has created Truth;
man is creating illusion.

Man does not realize that
he can create nothing real,
nor that God cannot create
anything that is unreal.

God
has never given man
the ability to
"make Real Things"
(Things of The Spirit),
but He has given him
the ability to
"make things (seem) real."

Man's most magical ability
is to "real-ize"
(make real to himself)
whatever he chooses,
be it Truth or illusion.

*Man tends to
judge a thing to be real
in direct relation
to the amount of energy
it creates within him.*

*But hate, fear, and anger
have never been real
because they have no life
outside what man provides.*

*When man withdraws his
"real-izing" force he will
see them dissolve to nothing.*

*The alchemist's age-old
dream was to magically
create "matter."*

*But every man has always
had an even more useful
ability to create "matter."*

*With his continual
"impositions of meaning"
man is always deciding,
for his own magical use,
what "matters" and
what doesn't "matter."*

*It is important
that Man become
fully aware of both
What He Truly Is,
and
what He is creating.*

*This is so He won't confuse
The
"Creative Self"
(Eternal Spirit)
with the
"self that He has created"
(time-bound personality).*

Thought
is perhaps
<u>the</u> most important thing
there is to think about.

For example:
the major difference
between
a man in Heaven
and
a man in hell,
is what
the man in Heaven
is <u>not</u> thinking about.

*You really don't need
more magical miracles
from God.*

*You need only
become more aware of the
amazing miracles that God
has already created.*

*Cling tightly
to the miracle that
YOU ARE !*

*True success in life
lies not in living longer,
for even the longest event
one day comes to an end;
but in living deeply.*

*If we live each moment
to it's fullest depth,
as if it could be the last,
length becomes unimportant.*

*In the depths of the moment
is where one sees and feels
It's Eternal Perfection.*

*As you choose to live
this magical life more
deeply and consciously,
an important question
to continually ask is:*

*In this moment,
"What am I making real,
what am I keeping real,"
knowing that if
I "drop it,"
I "stop it?"*

*As you choose to use
your creative magic,
as you choose to
consciously create your
"Heaven on Earth,"
become more fully aware
of the power of
your thoughts.*

*Become aware not only
of what your thoughts
are helping you to see,
but also of what they are
preventing you from seeing.*

*Think deeply
on these things:*

God,

Truth,

Beauty,

Love,

Light.

*Thank deeply
on these things.*

Now,
just for a minute,
try to grasp The Truth of
The Immense Intelligence,
Creativity, Time and Love
that has been necessary
for You to arrive at this
"present moment"
and this
"moment of presence."
Learn to rest completely
in this most amazing
Truth that Is Beyond Belief!